Your Daily Love Pill

Copyright 2017 © Your Daily Pill

All Rights Reserved

Spread across the following 365 pages are quotes on **love** – one for each day of the year. Think of each as your **daily love pill** intended to inspire, enlighten and warm the heart.

Love laughs at locksmiths.

Proverb

The magic of first love is our ignorance that it can never end.

Benjamin Disraeli

Never the time and the place and the loved one all together!

Robert Browning

To fear love is to fear life,
and those who fear life
are already three parts dead.

Bertrand Russell

Real love is a pilgrimage. It happens when there is no strategy, but it is very rare because most people are strategists.

Anita Brookner

I was nauseous and tingly all over.
I was either in love
or I had smallpox.

Woody Allen

Love thou the rose,
yet leave it on its stem.

Edward George Bulwer-Lytton

Life has taught us that love does not consist in gazing at each other but in looking outward together in the same direction.

Saint-Exupery

Love is everything. It is the key to life, and its influences are those that move the world.

Ralph Waldo Trine

The only abnormality is the incapacity to love.

Anais Nin

True love is the
parent of humility.

William Ellery Channing

In dreams and in love,
there are no impossibilities.

János Arnay

But it is impossible to replace
a person one has loved
with distractions.

Roald Dahl

Better to have lost and loved
than never to have loved at all.

Ernest Hemingway

True love makes the thought of death frequent, easy, without terrors; it merely becomes the standard of comparison, the price one would pay for many things.

Henri B. Stendhal

Who so loves
believes the impossible.

Elizabeth Barrett Browning

Love has no errors,
for all errors are the want for love.

William Law

Love is the wild card of existence.

Rita Mae Brown

The lover knows much more about absolute good and universal beauty than any logician or theologian, unless the latter, too, be lovers in disguise.

George Santayana

For small creatures such as we
the vastness is bearable
only through love.

Carl Sagan

Love is not just looking at each other, it's looking in the same direction.

Antoine de Saint-Exupery

Loving can cost a lot but not loving always costs more, and those who fear to love often find that want of love is an emptiness that robs the joy from life.

Merle Shan

Do not think that love in order to be genuine has to be extraordinary. What we need is to love without getting tired. Be faithful in small things because it is in them that your strength lies.

Mother Theresa

Love is quivering happiness.

Kahlil Gibran

Love is the only gold.

Alfred Lord Tennyson

Go to the truth beyond the mind.
Love is the bridge.

Stephen Levine

You may only be one person to the world, but you may also be the world to one person.

Anonymous

Looking back, I have this to regret, that too often when I loved, I did not say so.

David Grayson

Love is shown in your deeds,
not in your words.

Fr. Jerome Cummings

Love is the ability and willingness to allow those that you care for to be what they choose for themselves, without any insistence that they satisfy you.

Wayne Dyer

If you could only love enough, you could be the most powerful person in the world.

Emmet Fox

I love you not because of who you are, but because of who I am when I am with you.

Roy Croft

Where love is concerned,
too much is not even enough.

Pierre De Beaumarchais

You don't love someone for their looks, or their clothes, or for their fancy car, but because they sing a song only you can hear.

Oscar Wilde

Love is not in our choice
but in our fate.

John Dryden

Everyone of us needs to show how much we care for each other and, in the process, care for ourselves.

Princess of Wales Diana

The art of love is largely
the art of persistence.

Albert Ellis

I love you, not for what you are,
but for what I am
when I am with you.

Roy Croft

Love must be as much a light,
as it is a flame.

Henry David Thoreau

The cure for all ills and wrongs, the cares, the sorrows and the crimes of humanity, all lie in the one word 'love.' It is the divine vitality that everywhere produces and restores life.

Lydia Maria Child

People love others not for who they are, but for how they make them feel.

Irwin Federman

The bottom line is that (a) people are never perfect, but love can be, (b) that is the one and only way that the mediocre and vile can be transformed, and (c) doing that makes it that. We waste time looking for the perfect lover, instead of creating the perfect love.

Tom Robbins

Love is the poetry of the senses.

Anonymous

If I love you,
what business is it of yours?

Johann von Goethe

Do not seek the because – in love
there is no because, no reason,
no explanation, no solutions.

Anais Nin

In love the paradox occurs that
two beings become one
and yet remain two.

Erich Fromm

Love is an untamed force. When we try to control it, it destroys us. When we try to imprison it, it enslaves us. When we try to understand it, it leaves us feeling lost and confused.

Paulo Coelho

We are all born for love.
It is the principle of existence,
and its only end.

Benjamin Disraeli

When you love someone all your saved-up wishes start coming out.

Elizabeth Bowen

On the last analysis, then,
Love is life. Love never faileth
and life never faileth
so long as there is love.

Henry Drummond

Who loves, raves.

Lord Byron

You don't love because:
you love despite; not for the
virtues, but despite the faults.

William Faulkner

Nothing is more beautiful than the love that has weathered the storms of life. The love of the young for the young, that is the beginning of life. But the love of the old for the old, that is the beginning of things longer.

Jerome K. Jerome

Love is that condition in which the happiness of another person is essential to your own.

Robert A. Heinlein

Love talked about is easily turned aside, but love demonstrated is irresistible.

Stan Mooneyham

Real love stories
never have endings.

Richard Bach

Love is the total absence of fear.
Love asks no questions.
Its natural state is one of
extension and expansion, not
comparison and measurement.

Gerald G. Jampolsky

To love a thing
means wanting it to live.

Confucius

The two qualities which chiefly inspire regard and affection are that a thing is your own and that it is your only one.

Aristotle

When Death to either shall come
– I pray it be first to me.

Robert Bridges

Life in abundance comes only through great love.

Elbert Hubbard

If there's delight in love,
'Tis when I see that heart,
which others bleed for,
bleed for me.

William Congreve

True love is night jasmine,
a diamond in darkness,
the heartbeat no cardiologist has ever heard. It is the most common of miracles, fashioned of fleecy clouds – a handful of stars tossed into the night sky.

Jim Bishop

In real love you want the other person's good. In romantic love, you want the other person.

Margaret Anderson

The only thing we never get enough of is love; and the only thing we never give enough of is love.

Henry Miller

He who is in love is wise and is becoming wiser, sees newly every time he looks at the object beloved, drawing from it with his eyes and his mind those virtues which it possesses.

Ralph Waldo Emerson

Love is life's end, but never ending. Love is life's wealth, never spent, but ever spending. Love's life's reward, rewarded in rewarding.

Herbert Spencer

Love is composed of a single soul inhabiting two bodies.

Aristotle

Love is like a friendship caught on fire. In the beginning a flame, very pretty, often hot and fierce, but still only light and flickering. As love grows older, our hearts mature and our love becomes as coals, deep-burning and unquenchable.

Bruce Lee

Love makes everything that is heavy light.

Thomas Kempis

Life is the flower for which love is the honey.

Victor Hugo

Love cures people – both the ones who give it and the ones who receive it.

Karl Menninger

Love is just a system for getting someone to call you darling after sex.

Julian Barnes

Keep love in your heart. A life without it is like a sunless garden when the flowers are dead.

Oscar Wilde

The more connections you and
your lover make, not just
between your bodies,
but between your minds,
your hearts, and your souls,
the more you will strengthen the
fabric of your relationship,
and the more real moments
you will experience together.

Barbara De Angelis

The giving of love
is an education in itself.

Eleanor Roosevelt

If you love two people at the same time, choose the second. Because if you really loved the first one, you wouldn't have fallen for the second.

Johnny Depp

There exists, between people in love, a kind of capital held by each. This is not just a stock of affects or pleasure, but also the possibility of playing double or quits with the share you hold in the other's heart.

Jean Baudrillard

Many a man has fallen in love
with a girl in light so dim
he would not have chosen
a suit by it.

Maurice Chevalier

The pleasures of love are pains that become desirable, where sweetness and torment blend, and so love is voluntary insanity, infernal paradise, and celestial hell – in short, harmony of opposite yearnings, sorrowful laughter, soft diamond.

Umberto Eco

Love makes your soul crawl out from its hiding place.

Zora Neale Hurston

Love is the final end of the world's history,
the Amen of the universe.

Novalis Hardenberg

The supreme happiness in life is the conviction that we are loved.

Victor Hugo

Love in marriage should be the accomplishment of a beautiful dream, and not, as it too often is, the end.

Alphonse Karr

To get the full value of a joy
you must have somebody
to divide it with.

Mark Twain

Lovers don't finally meet somewhere. They're in each other all along.

Rumi

I was nauseous and tingly all over.
I was either in love
or I had smallpox.

Woody Allen

I am good, but not an angel.
I do sin, but I am not the devil.
I am just a small girl in a big world
trying to find someone to love.

Marilyn Monroe

Life without love is like a tree without blossoms or fruit.

Kahlil Gibran

What does love look like? It has the hands to help others. It has the feet to hasten to the poor and needy. It has eyes to see misery and want. It has the ears to hear the sighs and sorrows of men. That is what love looks like.

Saint Augustine of Hippo

A coward is incapable of exhibiting love; it is the prerogative of the brave.

Mahatma Gandhi

A flower cannot blossom
without sunshine,
and man cannot live without love.

Max Muller

We love the things we love
for what they are.

Robert Frost

The most important thing in life is to learn how to give out love, and to let it come in.

Morrie Schwartz

The greatest weakness of most humans is their hesitancy to tell others how much they love them while they're still alive.

Orlando A. Battista

You don't love someone for their looks, or their clothes, or for their fancy car, but because they sing a song only you can hear.

Oscar Wilde

Love and work are the cornerstones of our humanness.

Sigmund Freud

You will find as you look back upon your life that the moments when you have truly lived are the moments when you have done things in the spirit of love.

Henry Drummond

I argue thee that love is life.
And life hath immortality.

Emily Dickinson

To love and be loved is the great happiness of existence.

Sydney Smith

Ever has it been that love knows
 not its own depth until
 the hour of separation.

      Kahlil Gibran

Love loves to love love.

James Joyce

Love is never lost.
If not reciprocated,
it will flow back and soften
and purify the heart.

Washington Irving

One word frees us of all the
weight and pain of life;
that word is love.

Sophocles

Darkness cannot drive out
darkness: only light can do that.
Hate cannot drive out hate:
only love can do that.

Martin Luther King, Jr.

All, everything that I understand, I understand only because I love.

Leo Tolstoy

An act of love that fails is just as much a part of the divine life as an act of love that succeeds, for love is measured by fullness, not by reception.

Harold Lokes

Naturally, love's the most distant possibility.

Georges Bataille

We are shaped and fashioned
by what whom we love.

Johann von Goethe

Love and a cough cannot be hid.

George Herbert

There is no remedy for love
but to love more.

Henry David Thoreau

Don't hold to anger, hurt or pain.
They steal your energy and keep
you from love.

Leo Buscaglia

The greatest gift that you can give to others is the gift of unconditional love
and acceptance.

Brian Tracy

A man travels the world over in search of what he needs and returns home to find it.

George Moore

Love comes from blindness,
friendship from knowledge.

Comte DeBussy-Rabutin

Love seeks no cause beyond itself
and no fruit; it is its own fruit,
its own enjoyment.
I love because I love;
I love in order that I may love.

St. Bernard

If you have it Love, you don't
need to have anything else,
and if you don't have it, it doesn't
matter much what else you have.

James Barrie

Love is a given,
hatred is acquired.

Doug Horton

Sometimes the heart sees
what is invisible to the eye.

H. Jackson Brown, Jr.

Love is an irresistible desire
to be irresistibly desired.

Robert Frost

Someday, after mastering winds, waves, tides and gravity, we shall harness the energy of love; and for the second time in the history of the world, man will have discovered fire.

Pierre Teilhard de Chardin

Love is the great miracle cure. Loving ourselves works miracles in our lives.

Louise L. Hay

Love is when you meet someone who tells you something new about yourself.

Andre Breton

Do everything with so much love
in your heart that you would
never want to do it any other way.

Yogi Desai

Sympathy constitutes friendship; but in love there is a sort of antipathy, or opposing passion. Each strives to be the other, and both together make up one whole.

Samuel Taylor Coleridge

Oh love will make
a dog howl in rhyme.

Francis Beaumont

Love is all we have, the only way that each can help the other.

Euripides

Love is a promise;
love is a souvenir,
once given never forgotten,
never let it disappear.

John Lennon

The more I think about it,
the more I realize there is nothing
more artistic than to love others.

Vincent Van Gogh

Love is the voice under all silences, the hope which has no opposite in fear; the strength so strong mere force is feebleness: the truth more first than sun, more last than star.

E.E. Cummings

Love is an act of endless forgiveness, a tender look which becomes a habit.

Peter Ustinov

Love is the river of life
in the world.

Henry Ward Beecher

It is wrong to think that love comes from long companionship and persevering courtship. Love is the offspring of spiritual affinity and unless that affinity is created in a moment, it will not be created for years or even generations.

Kahlil Gibran

Love the giver more than the gift.

Brigham Young

Follow love and it will flee,
flee love and it will follow.

Proverb

This is the miracle that happens every time to those who really love; the more they give, the more they possess.

Rainer Maria Rilke

Love is friendship that has caught fire. It is quiet understanding, mutual confidence, sharing and forgiving. It is loyalty through good and bad times. It settles for less than perfection and makes allowances for human weaknesses.

Ann Landers

Absence sharpens love,
presence strengthens it.

Benjamin Franklin

Who travels for love finds a thousand miles not longer than one.

Japanese Proverb

We really have to understand the person we want to love. If our love is only a will to possess, it is not love. If we only think of ourselves, if we know only our own needs and ignore the needs of the other person,
we cannot love.

Thich Nhat Hanh

To fail to love is not to exist at all.

Mark Van Doren

Love is the immortal flow of energy that nourishes, extends and preserves. Its eternal goal is life.

Smiley Blanton

Love is something eternal;
the aspect may change,
but not the essence.

Vincent Van Gogh

It is by loving and by being loved that one can come nearest to the soul of another.

George McDonald

Love doesn't make the world go round. Love is what makes the ride worthwhile.

Franklin P. Jones

You can't blame gravity
for falling in love.

Albert Einstein

Nothing is impossible
for pure love.

Mahatma Gandhi

He who is not impatient
is not in love.

Italian Proverb

The highest function of love
is that it makes the loved one a
unique and irreplaceable being.

Tom Robbins

The love we give away
is the only love we keep.

Elbert Hubbard

You can't put a price tag on love,
but you can on all its accessories.

Melanie Clark

Love builds bridges
where there are none.

R. H. Delaney

Love is a better teacher
than duty.

Albert Einstein

Whenever you are confronted with an opponent. Conquer him with love.

Mahatma Gandhi

In the evening of life,
we will be judged on love alone.

Saint John of the Cross

Love is a force more formidable than any other. It is invisible – it cannot be seen or measured, yet it is powerful enough to transform you in a moment, and offer you more joy than any material possession could.

Barbara De Angelis

Love is a game that two can play and both win.

Eva Gabor

A heart that loves is always young.

Proverb

Love is the master key which opens the gates of happiness.

Oliver Wendell Holmes

The man who has never made a
fool of himself in love
will never be wise in love.

Theodor Reik

Love alone can unite living beings so as to complete and fulfill them... for it alone joins them by what is deepest in themselves. All we need is to imagine our ability to love developing until it embraces the totality of men and the earth.

Pierre Teilhard de Chardin

Love is but the discovery of ourselves in others, and the delight in the recognition.

Alexander Smith

Loving people live in a loving world. Hostile people live in a hostile world. Same world.

Wayne Dyer

Lovers who love truly do not write down their happiness.

Anatole France

For true love is inexhaustible; the more you give, the more you have. And if you go to draw at the true fountainhead, the more water you draw, the more abundant is its flow.

Antoine De Saint-Exupery

It is better to love wisely,
no doubt: but to love foolishly
is better than not to be able to
love at all.

William Makepeace Thackeray

The power of love, as the basis of a State, has never been tried.

Ralph Waldo Emerson

Where love rules, there is no will to power; where power predominates, there love is lacking. The one is the shadow of the other.

Carl Gustav Jung

Honor the ocean of love.

George De Benneville

Where we love is home,
home that our feet may leave,
but not our hearts.

Oliver Wendell Holmes

Pure love is a willingness to give without a thought of receiving anything in return.

Peace Pilgrim

Age does not protect you from love but love to some extent love protects you from age.

Jeanne Moreau

All thoughts, all passions,
all delights, Whatever stirs this
mortal frame, All are but ministers
of Love, And feed His
sacred flame.

Samuel Taylor Coleridge

If you would be loved, love, and be lovable.

Benjamin Franklin

The story of a love is not important – what is important is that one is capable of love. It is perhaps the only glimpse we are permitted of eternity.

Helen Hayes

Love is stronger than justice.

Sting

What the world really needs is more love and less paper work.

Pearl Bailey

For what is love itself, for the one we love best? An enfolding of immeasurable cares which yet are better than any joys outside our love.

George Eliot

Lots of people want to ride with you in the limo, but what you want is someone who will take the bus with you when the limo breaks down.

Oprah Winfrey

If you live to be a hundred,
I want to live to be a hundred
minus one day so I never
have to live without you.

A. A. Milne

The way to love anything is to realize that it might be lost.

Gilbert Keith Chesterton

I swear I couldn't love you more than I do right now, and yet I know I will tomorrow.

Leo Christopher

If you wish to be loved; Love!

Seneca

We love because it's the
only true adventure.

Nikki Giovanni

True love comes quietly, without banners or flashing lights. If you hear bells, get your ears checked.

Erich Segal

Love is the word used to label the sexual excitement of the young, the habituation of the middle-aged, and the mutual dependence of the old.

John Ciardi

Love is of all passions the strongest, for it attacks simultaneously the head, the heart and the senses.

Lao Tzu

Love is what is left in a relationship after all the selfishness is taken out.

Nick Richardson

Wicked men obey from fear;
good men, from love.

Aristotle

If you love something let it go free. If it doesn't come back, you never had it.
If it comes back, love it forever.

Doug Horton

When the power of love overcomes the love of power the world will know peace.

Jimi Hendrix

Love can neither be bought or sold, its only price is love.

Proverb

Love is life.
And if you miss love,
you miss life.

Leo Buscaglia

At the touch of love everyone becomes a poet.

Plato

You can give without loving, but you cannot love without giving.

Amy Carmichael

Love rules his kingdom
without a sword.

Proverb

If you were going to die soon and had only one phone call you could make, who would you call and what would you say? And why are you waiting?

Stephen Levine

The motto of chivalry is also the motto of wisdom; to serve all, but love only one.

Honore de Balzac

Love is love's reward.

John Dryden

Love gives naught but itself and takes naught but from itself. Love possesses not nor would it be possessed; For love is sufficient unto love.

Kahlil Gibran

It is better to have loved and lost than never to have lost at all.

Samuel Butler

There is only one happiness in this life, to love and be loved.

George Sand

We don't believe in rheumatism
and true love until
after the first attack.

Marie E. Eschenbach

The advantage of love at first sight is that it delays a second sight.

Natalie Clifford Barney

There is only one page left to
write on. I will fill it with words of
only one syllable. I love.
I have loved. I will love.

Audrey Niffenegger

Love consists of this:
two solitudes that meet,
protect and greet each other.

Rainer Maria Rilke

Love is the irresistible desire to be desired irresistibly.

Louis Ginsberg

Love is as much of an object as an obsession, everybody wants it, everybody seeks it, but few ever achieve it, those who do will cherish it, be lost in it, and among all, never... never forget it.

Curtis Judalet

To love without role, without power plays, is revolution.

Rita Mae Brown

We were two and had but one heart between us.

Francois de Montcorbier Villon

We love in another's soul
whatever of ourselves we can
deposit in it; the greater the
deposit, the greater the love.

Irving Layton

You come to love not by finding the perfect person,
but by seeing an imperfect person perfectly.

Sam Keen

However it is debased or misinterpreted, love is a redemptive feature. To focus on one individual so that their desires become superior to yours is a very cleansing experience.

Jeanette Winterson

Immature love says:
'I love you because I need you.'
Mature love says
'I need you because I love you.'

Erich Fromm

A successful marriage requires falling in love many times, always with the same person.

Mignon McLaughlin

Love is all you need.

The Beatles

Love and you shall be loved.
All love is mathematically just,
as much as the two sides
of an algebraic equation.

Ralph Waldo Emerson

Only from the heart
can you touch the sky.

Rumi

It is difficult to lay aside
a confirmed passion.

Catullus

Love never claims, it ever gives.
Love ever suffers, never resents
never revenges itself.

Mohandas K. Gandhi

Who, being loved, is poor?

Oscar Wilde

Love is a promise, love is a souvenir, once given never forgotten, never let it disappear.

John Lennon

There is no fear in love;
but perfect love casts out fear.

The Bible

You know you're in love when you don't want to fall asleep because reality is finally better than your dreams.

Dr. Seuss

The way is not in the sky.
The way is in the heart.

Buddha

I saw that you were perfect,
and so I loved you. Then I saw
that you were not perfect
and I loved you even more.

Angelita Lim

In this world of extremes,
we can only love too little.

Richard Cannarella

To love abundantly is to live abundantly, and to love forever is to live forever.

Henry Drummond

Love's greatest gift is its ability
to make everything it
touches sacred.

Barbara De Angelis

If you love somebody, let them go. If they return, they were always yours. If they don't, they never were.

Anonymous

The heart wants what it wants. There's no logic to these things. You meet someone and you fall in love and that's that.

Woody Allen

What is hell? I maintain that it is the suffering of being unable to love.

Fyodor Dostoyevsky

Love is an alliance of friendship and animalism; if the former predominates it is passion exalted and refined; if the latter, gross and sensual.

Charles Caleb Colton

Everything comes to us from others. To Be is to belong to someone.

Jean-Paul Sartre

Every day I live I am more convinced that the waste of life lies in the love we have not given, the powers we have not used, the selfish prudence that will risk nothing and which, shirking pain, misses happiness as well.

Mary Cholmondeley

I realized I was thinking of you, and I began to wonder how long you'd been on my mind. Then it occurred to me: Since I met you, you've never left.

Anonymous

There is always some madness in love. But there is also always some reason in madness.

Nietzsche

Love, while you are able to love.

A. Frieligrath

Love... Force it and it disappears. You cannot will love, nor even control it. You can only guide its expression. It comes or it goes according to those qualities in life that invite it or deny its presence.

David Seabury

Love is the last relay and ultimate outposts of eternity.

Dante Gabriel Rossetti

Women wish to be loved not
because they are pretty, or good,
or well bred, or graceful,
or intelligent, but because
they are themselves.

Henri Frederic Amiel

If it is your time, love will track you down like a cruise missile.

Lynda Barry

When I saw you I fell in love, and
you smiled because you knew.

William Shakespeare

Love is a great beautifier.

Louisa May Alcott

Love – the feeling –
is a fruit of love, the verb.

Stephen Covey

Love has nothing to do with what
you are expecting to get –
only with what you are expecting
to give – which is everything.

Katharine Hepburn

This world is full of beauty,
as other worlds above,
and if we did our duty,
it might be as full of love.

Gerald Massey

One is very crazy when in love.

Sigmund Freud

Better to have loved a short man than never to have loved a tall.

David Chambless

You don't love a woman because she is beautiful, but she is beautiful because you love her.

Anonymous

You talk too much, you laugh too loud, that's the price of love.

Brian Ferry

The supreme happiness in life is the conviction that we are loved – loved for ourselves, or rather, loved in spite of ourselves.

Victor Hugo

There is no remedy for love than to love more.

Henry David Thoreau

A very small degree of hope
is sufficient to cause
the birth of love.

Stendhal

I wish I could turn back the clock.
I'd find you sooner and
love you longer.

Anonymous

Love is the only sane and satisfactory answer to the problem of human existence.

Erich Fromm

Your task is not to seek for love,
but merely to seek and find all
the barriers within yourself that
you have built against it.

Rumi

A loving heart
is the truest wisdom.

Charles Dickens

It is a beautiful trait in the lover's character, that they think no evil of the object loved.

Henry Wadsworth Longfellow

Love is not measured by how many times you touch each other, but by how many times you reach each other.

Anonymous

He who love touches walks not in darkness.

Plato

Love is not to be purchased,
and affection has no price.

St. Jerome

A proof that experience is of no use, is that the end of one love does not prevent us from beginning another.

Paul Bourget

It makes no difference how
deeply seated may be the trouble,
how hopeless the outlook,
how muddled the tangle,
how great the mistake.
A sufficient realization of love
will dissolve it all.

Emmet Fox

There is no love without forgiveness, and there is no forgiveness without love.

Bryant H. McGill

People who are sensible about love are incapable of it.

Douglas Yates

The fate of love is that it always seems too little or too much.

Amelia E. Barr

Love is a canvas furnished
by nature and embroidered
by imagination.

Voltaire

Love is the greatest refreshment in life.

Pablo Picasso

A man in love mistakes
a pimple for a dimple.

Japanese Proverb

Love; it will not betray you,
dismay or enslave you.
It will set you free.

Mumford & Sons

There is a madness in loving you, a lack of reason that makes it feel so flawless.

Leo Christopher

Who can give law to lovers?
Love is a greater law to itself.

Boethius

It is easier to guard a sack full of fleas than a girl in love.

Yiddish Proverb

Love is a conflict between reflexes and reflections.

Mangnu Hirschfield

Do you want to know a good way to fall in love? Just associate with all your pleasant experiences with someone, and disassociate from all the unpleasant ones.

Richard Bandler

Is it not by love alone that we succeed in penetrating to the very essence of being?

Igor Stravinsky

Love is the affinity which links
and draws together the elements
of the world... Love, in fact,
is the agent of universal synthesis.

Pierre Teilhard de Chardin

Love does not begin and end the way we seem to think it does. Love is a battle, love is a war; love is a growing up.

James Baldwin

True love cannot be found where it truly does not exist, nor can it be hidden where it truly does.

Anonymous

Love means to love that which is unlovable; or it is no virtue at all.

G. K. Chesterton

Love is not blind - it sees more, not less. But because it sees more, it is willing to see less.

Rabbi J. Gordon

Love, by its very nature, is unworldly, and it is for this reason rather than its rarity that it is not only apolitical but anti-political, perhaps the most powerful of all anti-political human forces.

Hannah Arendt

Lovers are fools,
but Nature makes them so.

Elbert Hubbard

The richest love is that which
submits to the arbitration of time.

Lawrence Durrell

For a crowd is not company; and faces are but a gallery of pictures; and talk but a tinkling cymbal, where there is no love.

Francis Bacon

Love is blind.

Chaucer

Love poems are always cliche to me but not to the person it's for.

James Dye

Most people would rather give than get affection.

Aristotle

I never knew how to worship
until I knew how to love.

Henry Ward Beecher

Have enough courage
to trust love one more time
and always one more time.

Maya Angelou

We who were loved will never unlive that crippling fever.

Adrienne Rich

One word frees us of all the weight and pain of life:
That word is love.

Sophocles

Treasure the love you receive above all. It will survive long after your good health has vanished.

Og Mandino

To try to write love is to confront the muck of language: that region of hysteria where language is both too much and too little, excessive and impoverished.

Roland Barthes

You don't love someone because they're perfect, you love them in spite of the fact that they're not.

Jodi Picoult

The best proof of love is trust.

Joyce Brothers

I don't want to live – I want to love first, and live incidentally.

Zelda Fitzgerald

Love is the bridge between two hearts.

Anonymous

Sometimes, when one person is missing, the whole world seems depopulated.

Alphonse De Lamartine

Love is not love until
love's vulnerable.

Theodore Roethke

Love can never grow old. Locks may lose their brown and gold. Cheeks may fade and hollow grow. But the hearts that love will know, never winter's frost and chill, summer's warmth is in them still.

Leo Buscaglia

Love isn't something you find.
Love is something that finds you.

Loretta Young

There is love of course.
And then there's life, its enemy.

Jean Anouilh

He that plants trees loves others besides himself.

English Proverb

Who is wise in love,
love most, say least.

Alfred Lord Tennyson

Love is like the wind, you can't see it, but you can feel it.

Nicholas Sparks

Love takes off masks that we fear we cannot live without and know we cannot live within.

James Baldwin

Love comes when manipulation stops; when you think more about the other person than about his or her reactions to you. When you dare to reveal yourself fully. When you dare to be vulnerable.

Joyce Brothers

One is loved because one is loved.
No reason is needed for loving.

Paulo Coelho

Love is like an hourglass, with the heart filling up as the brain empties.

Jules Renard

Love is a friendship set to music.

Joseph Campbell

Love is, above all,
the gift of oneself.

Jean Anouilh Ardele

Let the lover be disgraceful, crazy, absent-minded. Someone sober will worry about events going badly. Let the lover be.

Rumi

It is easy to halve the potato where there is love.

Proverb

Love seeketh not itself to please, nor for itself hath any care, but for another gives its ease, and builds a Heaven in Hell's despair.

William Blake

Love is the only force capable of transforming an enemy into friend.

Martin Luther King, Jr.

To love is nothing. To be loved is something. But to love and be loved, that's everything.

T. Tolis

To be fully seen by somebody, then, and be loved anyhow – this is a human offering that can border on miraculous.

Elizabeth Gilbert

The sweetest joy,
the wildest woe is love.

Pearl Bailey

Love is most nearly itself when here and now cease to matter.

T.S. Eliot

All you need is love.
But a little chocolate
now and then doesn't hurt.

Charles Schulz

Love is not only something you feel. It's something you do.

David Wilkerson

Love does not consist in gazing at each other, but in looking outward together in the same direction.

Antoine De Saint-Exupery

Accept the things to which fate binds you, and love the people with whom fate brings you together, but do so with all your heart.

Marcus Aurelius

Where there is love there is life.

Mahatma Gandhi

Love is misunderstood to be an emotion; actually, it is a state of awareness, a way of being in the world, a way of seeing oneself and others.

David R. Hawkins

Love – a wildly misunderstood
although highly desirable
malfunction of the heart
which weakens the brain,
causes eyes to sparkle,
cheeks to glow,
blood pressure to rise
and the lips to pucker

Anonymous

The pain of love is
the pain of being alive.
It is a perpetual wound.

Maureen Duffy

It is difficult to know at what
moment love begins;
it is less difficult to know
that it has begun.

Henry Wadsworth Longfellow

There is no remedy for love,
but to love more.

Thoreau

The minute I heard my first love story I started looking for you, not knowing how blind that was. Lovers don't finally meet somewhere. They're in each other all along.

Rumi

Love one another and you will be happy. It's as simple and as difficult as that.

Michael Leunig

If love is shelter,
I'm going to walk in the rain.

Anonymous

In a great romance, each person plays a part the other really likes.

Elizabeth Ashley

Woe to the man whose heart has not learned while young to hope, to love – and to put its trust in life.

Joseph Conrad

Love is not altogether a delirium, yet it has many points in common therewith.

Thomas Carlyle

Love is not a matter of counting the years –
it's making the years count.

Wolfman Jack Smith

Love possesses not nor will it be possessed, for love is sufficient unto love.

Kahlil Gibran

I have found the paradox that if I love until it hurts, then there is no hurt, but only more love.

Mother Theresa

Gravitation is not responsible for people falling in love.

Albert Einstein

Love is said to be blind,
but I know some fellows in love
who can see twice as much
in their sweethearts as I do.

Josh Billings

To love one person with a private love is poor and miserable: to love all is glorious.

Thomas Traherne

Love is much like a wild rose, beautiful and calm, but willing to draw blood in its defense.

Mark Overby

Love is the joy of the good,
the wonder of the wise,
the amazement of the Gods.

Plato

I would rather live and love where death is king than have eternal life where love is not.

Robert G. Ingersoll

You are my lover and I am your mistress and kingdoms and empires and governments have tottered and succumbed before now to that mighty combination.

Violet Trefusis

We're all a little weird, and life's a little weird. And when we find someone whose weirdness is compatible with ours, we join up with them and fall in mutual weirdness and call it love.

Dr. Seuss

As for me, to love you alone,
to make you happy, to do nothing
which would contradict your
wishes, this is my destiny
and the meaning of my life.

Napoleon Bonaparte

Love alone could waken love.

Pearl Buck

Love sought is good,
but given unsought is better.

William Shakespeare

Not all of us have to possess earthshaking talent. Just common sense and love will do.

Myrtle Auvil

When love is not madness it is not love.

Pedro Calderón de la Barca

I have decided to stick with love.
Hate is too great a burden to bear.

Martin Luther King, Jr.

Love is like war: easy to begin but very hard to stop.

H. L. Mencken

Everyone admits that love is wonderful and necessary, yet no one agrees on just what it is.

Diane Ackerman

Sex alleviates tension.
Love causes it.

Woody Allen

We love but once,
for once only are we perfectly
equipped for loving.

Cyril Connolly

The hunger for love
is much more difficult to remove
than the hunger for bread.

Mother Theresa

Talk not of wasted affection; affection never was wasted.

Henry Wadsworth Longfellow

It is at the edge of a petal
that love waits.

William Carlos Williams

Nobody has ever measured,
not even poets,
how much the heart can hold.

Zelda Fitzgerald

To love and be loved is to feel the sun from both sides.

David Viscott

Love is a mutual self-giving which ends in self-recovery.

Fulton J. Sheen

And in the end, the love you take,
is equal to the love you make.

The Beatles

To see the list of other Your Daily Pill books on different topics, visit **www.yourdailypill.com**

www.ingramcontent.com/pod-product-compliance
Lightning Source LLC
Chambersburg PA
CBHW031404290426
44110CB00011B/256